Words
Of Wisdom
& Inspiration

Jim Rogahn

Scripture taken from the New King James Version. Copyright © 1982 by Thomas Nelson, Inc. Used by permission. All rights reserved.

Copyright © 2017 Jim Rogahn

www.jimrogahn.org

All rights reserved

ISBN-10:1978012330
ISBN-13:978-1978012332

Preface

At one time or another, sooner or later, we will all need some wisdom and inspiration. We live in a world that too often is negative, confused, and difficult to deal with. One goal that I have in life is to be a source of encouragement and strength to others, to help people find the right direction for their life, and to help them learn how to successfully follow that course.

Some of the things written in this book may contribute to an idea you already have and help you move forward with it. Some of the things in this book may give you the encouragement you have been looking for to take that next step in life, or to keep on going. Whatever the case, I pray that in some way you benefit and are made better by the words of wisdom and inspiration found in this book.

Romans 8:14 (NKJV) "For as many as are led by the Spirit of God, these are sons of God."

Christians should be led by the Spirit of God. He lives in us and He will guide us and direct us in life.

Believers are not led by feelings, open or closed doors, traditions, other people's opinions, or circumstances. Every child of God needs to learn how to be led by the Spirit of God.

How do we learn to hear God's voice? A good place to start is in the Word of God, which the Holy Spirit guided men to write (2 Peter 1:20-21).

The Spirit of God will speak to us through the Word of God, that is a good way to begin to learn how to be led.

All Christians may not always agree with each other, but all Christians must agree with the Bible.

God is working today to put into us, and to get to us, the things that we will need for success tomorrow.

No one looks back at their life and wishes that they had done less for God.

Being made righteous simply means being made right. Through Jesus, we become righteous and right with God because Jesus took the penalty of sin for us (2 Corinthians 5:21).

We cannot earn our right standing with God, nothing we do will make us more righteous; being made right with God only comes through faith in Jesus.

God's Word is always valid and relevant.

Romans 10:17 (NKJV) "So then faith comes by hearing, and hearing by the word of God."

It is important for every believer to hear and keep on hearing the Word of God to build and strengthen our faith.

We need to take advantage of opportunities we have to hear good teaching and preaching to keep ourselves strong in faith.

If you focus on yourself and your abilities you will always be limited in what you can do for God.

But, if you focus on the Greater One, the Holy Spirit, in you – He has no limits, and He will help you do whatever God calls you to do, and to do whatever needs to be done.

God's Word is given to us to help us grow. If you don't know the Word you won't grow (1 Peter 2:2).

One of the greatest needs among Christians today is to get to know God's Word and to make it the foundation for their life.

There is no substitute for the Word of God in the life of a believer.

When we receive Jesus into our life we become a new creation in Christ (2 Corinthians 5:17); all the old is gone and we are made new!

I am not who I used to be, now I am a new creation with a new life and a new purpose. All the mistakes and failures of the past are gone and my future is bright!

You can know all the facts and still not understand the truth.

Just because we come to an open door it does not mean that we are supposed to walk through it.

Just because we have an opportunity to do something does not mean we should do it.

Just because we can follow a certain path does not mean that we should take it.

Just because something looks or feels right does not mean that it is.

We must follow the direction we have from God's Word and be led by the Holy Spirit to make right choices in life.

Some people are more familiar with the story of their life and what they have done than they are with the story of the life of Jesus and what He has done.

We have a choice as to what we will consider and focus on, what Jesus has done or what we have done.

God's Word's is what we need to show us the right things to believe, to help us avoid error, to correct us, and to guide us in our life (2 Timothy 3:16).

Scripture was given to us so we would be complete (mature) and equipped for all that God has called us to do (2 Timothy 3:17).

We need to be sure that we are spending time reading and studying God's Word to be developed and properly equipped to do the will of God.

We can't control everything that happens around us, but no matter what happens we can choose to walk in the wisdom of God, focus on, and speak His Word.

What people want is often not what they really need.

We live in an age of information overload, and much of the information we receive is not good, helpful, or accurate.

Speculation and guessing are not proper ways to interpret the Bible.

Many Christians are wondering how to find and fulfill the will of God for their life. Here is the answer.
1. Get a Bible
2. Read the Bible
3. Do what the Bible says to do
4. Continue to repeat this process

Congratulations, you have discovered how to fulfill God's plan for your life.

We find the general will of God in the Bible. As we continue to do the general will of God, God will lead us from His overall, general will for our life into His specific plans and purposes. If we cannot even do the basics of the will of God, as found in God's Word, it will be difficult for us to move forward in His specific plan for our life.

It is not what the Bible says that confuses people.

It is what people claim that the Bible says, and what people say about the Bible, that confuses people.

Following the Word of God and the leading of the Holy Spirit in our life will bring us into and keep us in the place of success and peace.

Following the flesh and/or the intellect will bring us into and keep us in the place of confusion, frustration, and trouble.

Where we are today is a result of what we have been following.

It is also good to know it is really never too late to change what we follow and pay attention to.

Many Christians are waiting for a feeling or an experience to move them to do something.

Christians should be motivated by the Holy Spirit and the Word of God, not feelings or experiences.

If someone is always thinking about the wrong things and talking about the wrong things it is no surprise if they struggle with stress, anxiety, and depression.

Changing your thinking and your words to line up with God's Word will change your life!

Our level of success in life will be directly related to how much of what we do, think, and say is in line with God's Word and His plan for our life.

The farther you get away from the truth and light in God's Word the more you will get into deception, confusion, and just plain foolishness.

John 10:10 (NKJV) "The thief does not come except to steal, and to kill, and to destroy. I have come that they may have life, and that they may have it more abundantly.

I am so happy that Jesus came to help us to have the best life possible and give us a reason for living.

The devil wants to ruin our life, but God's plan for each and every one of us is to have an abundant life. I choose to follow Jesus and live an abundant life!

Our feelings do not make the Word of God more or less true, valid, or effective.

Luke 4:16 (NKJV) "So He came to Nazareth, where He had been brought up. And as His custom was, He went into the synagogue on the Sabbath day, and stood up to read."

Jesus was and is the Son of God. Jesus was far more spiritually mature and in tune with God than any other person while He was here on the earth, and still, it was His "custom", His habit, to go to the synagogue on the Sabbath day.

If it was a good idea for Jesus to get together on a regular basis with other like-minded people, then it is probably a good idea for Christians to do the same thing.

It's better to be a doer of the Word than just a talker about the Word.

If we do what is right in the easy places, when things are good and all is well, it will be easier for us to do what is right in the hard places, when things are not going so good.

All of us will face difficulties and challenges in life; what we do today will help us to be an overcomer tomorrow, or it will allow us to be overcome.

It is interesting how often in the Book of Proverbs we see things like:
- Incline your ear to wisdom
- Get wisdom
- Receive instruction
- Hear instruction
- Keep sound wisdom
- Take firm hold of instruction
- Keep instruction

Repeatedly we are told to do something to obtain wisdom and instruction. But most people don't do that, so when they have a problem they want to receive a "miracle" to get out of their problem.

If we would take advantage of the wisdom and instruction made available to us through God's Word and through good, biblical teaching, we would avoid many problems and have the understanding about what to do with those problems that we do experience.

We need to watch for the wisdom and instruction God brings to us, receive it, and act on it!

Anything that takes your focus off of the work that God did for you through Jesus and puts it on your own works is leading you away from the truth of God's Word.

Yield, obey, and submit are three words that many people do not like, but they are three important words for spiritual growth and success.

All believers need to:
- Yield to the Holy Spirit by following His direction (Romans 8:14).
- Obey the Word of God by being a doer of the Word (James 1:22).
- Submit to good spiritual leaders by allowing them to speak into our life (Hebrews 13:17)

By following the direction of the Holy Spirit, acting on the Word of God, and allowing those God has placed over us to help us, we will be strong, mature believers who will do great things for God.

How we react to the things that happen around us and to us will determine how fast and how far we go forward with God.

Christians should be governed by inward convictions based on the Word of God and not ruled by outward pressure from circumstances or other people.

You lose your joy when you focus on your circumstances.

Some people speak but really have nothing to say.

Some people speak but their words do not need to be heard.

Some people speak and have something to say that everyone needs to hear.

Who we choose to listen to is very important, so we must choose wisely who we listen to.

Just because we find an open door it does not mean that we need to enter that place.

Just because we find a closed door it does not mean that we should leave that place.

God leads us by the Holy Spirit, not open or closed doors.

We need wisdom and direction from the Holy Spirit to know when to walk away, when to knock, and when to use the keys we already have to open doors.

Proverbs 13:3 (NKJV) "He who guards his mouth preserves his life, but he who opens wide his lips shall have destruction."

Some people want to blame circumstances, the devil, or even other people for their problems, but they are really just destroying themselves by saying the wrong things.

Find out what God's Word has to say about you, your life, and your situation and speak God's Word. That is how you "preserve" your life!

The physical position you take in prayer, the eloquence of your speech, and the volume of your voice do not increase or decrease the effectiveness of your prayers.

For our prayers to be effective they must be based on God's Word.

Many believers are looking for someone or something outside of themselves for help.

Instead of looking to the outside, we should be looking inside for help and direction from the Holy Spirit.

You can get more accomplished in five minutes with God's help and following His direction than you can in five hours, or even five days, trying to do it all on your own and relying on your own wisdom.

Direction and purpose fit well together.

Direction is: guidance, the course something is moving, a channel of thought or action.

Purpose is: something set up as an object or an end to be obtained, an intention.

When you have direction, there is purpose; where there is purpose, you have direction.

When you lack direction, there is no purpose; when you lack purpose, there is no direction.

Some Christians are very good at telling you what they are against, what they don't agree with, and what they don't believe in.

It would be better if we would tell people what we believe in, why we believe it, and what our standard in life is instead of repeatedly bringing up the negative side of things.

Some ministers say that their teaching is deep and complicated, and that is why some people don't understand it.

The reality of it is that these ministers are usually just getting away from the simplicity of God's Word.

We should not gauge our level of success on what others are doing or have done.

Our success or failure is based on whether or not we are following God's plan for our life and being doers of the Word, no matter how our lives may look compared to other people.

We will be far more successful if we build our doctrine on what we find in and then bring out of the Bible, than if we create our doctrine and try to put it into the Bible and find verses to justify our beliefs.

Things that fascinate your mind, stimulate your curiosity, or stir your emotions will not necessarily help develop your spirit.

Your actions, attitudes, and the words you speak will have a greater impact and influence on your life than anything anyone else might do to you or for you, think about you, or say to you or about you.

There are many things that you can have too much of and it would be harmful to you.

But one thing you cannot have too much of is the Bible.

Many Christians say things like:
- If I was the pastor I would (or would not) ...
- If I was the leader of the group I would (or would not) ...
- If I was the person leading the praise and worship here I would (or would not) ...
- Etc., etc.

It seems that many people that God never called to do something know all the answers about how that thing should be done.

It would be better if we all focus on what God has called us to do and not get involved in trying to direct someone else in the work that God has called them to.

What Jesus did was not something that was separate from who He was, it was a part of Him.

What we do for God should be a reflection of our relationship with God.

There are times when we face difficulties that it seems like we don't know what to do in the present and the future looks dim.

That's when it's a good time to reflect on God's Word and the victories that God has given us in the past. God does not change and what He did before He can and will do again.

God's future for us is bright and His plan for us is always victory and success!

It amazes me how many ministers focus on and talk about minor points found in the Bible, or even worse, things that are just suggested in the Bible, while almost completely ignoring the major issues that are found repeatedly throughout the Bible.

We must focus on the major doctrines of the Bible to build a stable Christian life for ourselves and to help others do the same.

The direction you are traveling is more important than the speed you are going.

They used to say, "If a tree falls in a forest and no one is there to hear it, does it make a sound?"

Now we could say, "If someone does something good but no one posts it on Facebook, Tweets about it, or puts in on Instagram, etc. does it matter?"

The answer, at least for the second question, is a definite yes. Everything we do for God is seen by Him and is valuable in His eyes even if no one likes it, comments about it, or it becomes a trending topic.

Don't gauge the success of your life or ministry on whether or not any person knows or understands what you are doing or have done. It matters more what God thinks about what we are doing than what anyone else thinks.

Just because you want something to be true, you feel strongly about it, or it stirs you emotionally, does not make it true, right, or good.

Acts 27:25 (NKJV) "Therefore take heart, men, for I believe God that it will be just as it was told me."

Paul said this when he was on a ship that was going through a terrible storm. The storm was so bad that the people on board, including the professional sailors, "lost all hope of being saved".

Paul told everyone to "take heart" (to be of good cheer, to have good courage) because God had told Paul that they would make it through the storm.

No matter what storms may come, no matter what the experts might believe or say, no matter how things look or how you feel in the situation, do like Paul did and believe what God has said.

Standing in faith on God's Word will lead you through, and out of, the storm every time!

There are a lot of things you can substitute and use in place of something else, like sugar substitutes, butter substitutes, salt substitutes, and egg substitutes.

But, there is nothing you can use in place of the Bible; there is no substitute for God's Word.

God does not lead Christians by guilt, fear, needs, or external pressure.

Every Christian should be led by the Holy Spirit and the Word of God, in every area of life.

No matter how dark your past may have been there is always a bright future with God.

It continually amazes me that so many ministers rely heavily on verses from the Old Testament, and even the Gospels, to build their doctrine while almost completely ignoring the Epistles, the letters written to the Church.

Certainly, the Old Testament and the Gospels have value for us today. But, we are New Covenant believers and the letters to the Church are where we should put our main focus, without neglecting the truths found in the Old Testament and the Gospels.

Your success or failure in life has more to do with what you do than with what other people have done, are doing, or can do for you.

No matter what the devil tries to put into your path to stop you, don't let his attempts to restrict you become the limits in your life.

God never called anyone to be average; God calls us and equips us to do great things for Him.

There is something I have noticed when reading the Bible that maybe other people have not seen.

When I read things like:
- Go into all the world and preach the Gospel (Mark 16:15)
- Serve one another in love (Galatians 5:13)
- Be kind to one another, tenderhearted, forgiving (Ephesians 4:32)
- Continue earnestly in prayer (Colossians 4:2)
- Don't forsake meeting together (Hebrews 10:25)

I have noticed that none of those verses include the words, "When you feel like it" or "When it fits into your schedule". Maybe I use a different translation of the Bible than other people do, or maybe people have misunderstood something that is in the Bible.

I once heard a minister teach about a certain topic. He used some Old Testament verses and an example from his own life when teaching about this subject.

He then said that he had "proved" this doctrine through his use of a couple of Old Testament verses and his personal example. But, that is not good enough to "prove" anything.

We cannot build New Testament doctrine with only Old Testament verses and personal stories.

If we do not have any verses from the New Testament, if Jesus did not talk about the subject and Paul, John, Peter, James, and even Jude did not teach about it, then it is probably not a New Testament doctrine.

You cannot build a sound, biblical doctrine on just one Bible verse. But, when you build sound, biblical doctrine you cannot ignore any Bible verse.

The whole Bible fits together in agreement, and if one verse clearly contradicts our doctrine then we need to reexamine what we believe in the light of the whole Bible.

We need to know the entire Bible to build accurate Bible doctrines.

Wisdom is not just knowing what to say and when to say it, wisdom is also knowing what not to say and when not to say it.

If we want to have a "sound mind" then we need to have the right sound in our mind.

We must choose to think God's thoughts, speak God's Word, and be sure that we are hearing the right things.

Wrong words bring wrong ideas that can create problems in our thinking.

John 12:42-43 (NKJV) "Nevertheless even among the rulers many believed in Him, but because of the Pharisees they did not confess Him, lest they should be put out of the synagogue; for they loved the praise of men more than the praise of God."

Who we seek to please and earn the praise of says a lot about where we are in our walk with God.

We should make it our goal to do things that please our heavenly Father, even if it does not please our earthly friends.

It is always good for us to go to God's Word and then base our beliefs on what we find in the Bible.

It is never a good idea for us to take our beliefs and see how we can fit them into the Bible.

God can use everyone in some way to help someone else.

You are the somebody that someone else needs.

Recently I saw a minister on "Christian TV" talking about how they were going to "speak things into the lives" of the people watching so that those people could have the things that God wants them to have.

It does not matter what any minister says or declares about you or your life, who prays for you, how many people lay hands on you, or whatever else happens if you don't do what the Word of God says you need to do.

The people who are doers of the Word are the people who are blessed and walk in God's best, not the people that someone spoke over, prayed for, laid hands on, etc.

Too many ministers make their teaching so complicated that they end up being the only ones that seem to understand what they are talking about.

The goal should be that what we teach and preach is simple enough for people to get a hold of it and put it into practice in their lives.

Our emotions and experiences do not overrule God's Word.

We must keep God's Word as our highest authority.

The Bible says that greater is He that is in us, the Holy Spirit, than he that is in the world (1 John 4:4) and that no weapon formed against us will prosper (Isaiah 54:17).

As believers, the Holy Spirit is inside of us and the things that come against us are on the outside of us.

Strength, wisdom, and guidance from the Holy Spirit on the inside will help us to have victory over whatever comes against us from the outside.

There are many things you can find that are flexible or pliable, and they can be stretched to fit whatever you like or shaped into whatever you want.

God's Word is not one of those things. You have to take what the Word says for what it says and not try to stretch it to cover what you want or form it into something you want it to be.

When we face a difficult situation, or there are problems in our life, we don't need to see what our family says about it, what our friends say about it, what the government says about it, or what society says about it. We need to find out what the Bible says about it and respond accordingly.

If you look hard enough you are sure to find something that will offend you.

And if you look hard enough you can also be sure to find a reason not to be offended.

It is easier to be offended than it is to overlook an offense and stay focused on what is really important, but avoiding being offended is a far better way to live.

Christians are a part of the Body of Christ (1 Corinthians 12:27).

There are no extra, useless, or unnecessary parts in the Body of Christ.

God has a plan and purpose for each and every person; our goal in life should be to find and fulfill God's plan and to follow His purpose.

Just because someone has a public forum to speak does not mean that what they say is worth listening to.

Choose who you listen to and be a discerning listener, don't just believe or accept everything you hear.

If you know more about what others have said about God's Word than you actually know God's Word, then there is a problem.

Basing our life on the truth of the Bible will lead us to success, basing our life on something else will lead to disappointment and failure.

When we pray according to God's Word we can, and should, expect results.

Many people fail to do great things for God, but not because they lack the opportunity.

Some people fail because when the opportunity to do something great for God comes they are not ready to take advantage of that opportunity.

Other people fail to do great things for God because they are not willing to pay the price associated with the opportunity.

We like to think our success is completely in God's hands, but we need to do our part to be prepared and to be willing to obey when God brings an opportunity to us.

Some people are waiting for others to find a way to make them fit into an already existing situation and to adapt things to them as they are now.

It would be better and wiser if each person would take what they have, where they are now, and find a way to contribute it to something bigger than themselves.

Some people who struggle with problems say that they don't have time to read their Bible, pray, and go to church every week.

But, it seems that most of these same people do have time for many other things in their life.

So, the real issue is not the amount of time that is available, but it is a matter of priorities and how we spend our time.

When we get our priorities in order it will help us to get our life in order and spend our time wisely.

Just because you can do something, or you want to do something, does not mean you should do it.

No matter how wonderful, interesting, or exciting some teaching sounds, if it is not based on clear Bible verses we cannot accept it as doctrine.

We must build our foundation for life on what the Bible really teaches, or we will never really be able to stand in our place in life to fulfill the will of God.

If you can't swim, you can't help someone who is drowning.

Too many Christians don't really know much about the Bible and as a result their lives are a mess. In this condition, those Christians are not really going to be much help to anyone else.

Learn to "swim" and God will be able to use you to help others.

Sometimes when we find ourselves under pressure is it simply our dealing with all of the issues and challenges that we face in life.

God can help us overcome in these situations so that we can walk in victory.

Sometimes when we are under pressure it is because we are in the wrong place and/or we are doing the wrong thing(s).

In these situations, we need to follow the counsel of God's Word and the leading of the Holy Spirit to move to the place where we ought to be and to do the things we ought to do.

The key in either situation is knowing what God's Word has to say and always listening to the wisdom and direction of God through the Holy Spirit.

Often the people who act like they know the most seem to do the least.

There are some who want to be experts at something without ever doing anything.

There are times when we are looking for some big thing to happen to bring a change or meet a need in our life.

But, the reality is that usually we just need to keep on doing the things we know that God has given us to do and keep on going the direction He has shown us to go until we know otherwise.

Faithfully doing the things that God has called us to do and acting on His Word will bring us the success that we are looking for.

There is no such thing as unemployment in the Body of Christ.

There are many things that God wants to do and He is looking for someone to step up and do those things.

What can you do? What should you do? What will you do?

One main rule of Bible interpretation is that Scripture interprets Scripture.

We should not interpret Scripture based on current events, our circumstances, or past experience.

Faith and wisdom are not opposites.

You cannot overrule wisdom through faith.

Just because something is interesting, exciting, or entertaining does not mean that it is biblical, helpful, or good.

Romans 8:14 (NKJV) "For as many as are led by the Spirit of God, these are sons of God."

Children of God need to be led by their Heavenly Father, He does this by the Holy Spirit working in us.

It is always good when the Father leads His children, when children lead children it can lead to trouble.

In all the years that I have been a Christian, and especially since I have been in full-time ministry, I have never met a person and thought, "They know too much about the Bible".

The good news is that this is something that is easy to fix, just start reading the Bible and keep on reading it.

Act on what the Bible says, think about what it says, and talk about what it says. Your life will be better for doing so.

Taking steps to follow the plan of God is easy when you go one step at a time.

It is when you try to take two or three steps at once that it gets difficult.

Take the next step that God gives you in life and ministry and don't be so concerned about the steps after that.

Just go one step at a time and you will be fine.

It's nice to know that the Word of God and everything God provided for us through Jesus does not have an expiration date.

Stepping into the call of God also means stepping into God's provision.

As God calls us He also supplies what is necessary for us to fulfill that call.

Whatever God is calling you to do in life, follow His direction and He will guide you and provide for you.

As we step out in faith doing what we know to do, and using what we have, God will always be there to help us and to give us further direction about what to do next.

In Mark 11, Jesus said that we need to speak to the mountain, symbolizing whatever challenge or problem we may be facing, and command it to leave, to be cast into the sea

Jesus did not say to talk about, analyze or describe the mountain, tell all your friends about the mountain, or go live on the mountain (or under it), it seems like some people have gotten that mixed up.

Find out what God's Word says and speak that to the mountain.

The love of God and unconditional acceptance are not the same thing.

It would be great if every time a Christian, and especially a minister, states, "The Bible says ..." that it was actually something the Bible does say.

Steps of obedience in the will and plan of God lead to success. Failing to take those steps of obedience leads to frustration and failure.

If God is giving us direction to do something or change something then we need to follow that direction and obey.

God knows better than we do what we need, where we should go, and how to do what we need to do; we must obey His direction to achieve our goals.

It is our responsibility to search the Scriptures to know the truth of the Word for ourselves and not to just rely on what others tell us the Bible says.

A statement of fact is only that because there is some truth to back up what is said.

Just because someone says something is true does not make their statement factual.

Just because something is repeated often, or said loudly, or said with emotion, also does not mean that what is said is true.

There has to be some basis for what is said, some foundation that it is built on, you can't just say something and claim that it's the truth.

A good place to start is with God's Word, because we know it is the truth.

Psalm 119:160 (NKJV) "The entirety of Your word is truth, and every one of Your righteous judgments endures forever."

Paul told Timothy, in 2 Timothy 2:17-18, that the faith of some people was overthrown by what other people were saying. What some people believed, first of all, caused them to stray from the truth and then that wrong belief had an effect on others, through words.

Our words can help to strengthen our faith and the faith of those around us, or our words can overthrow the faith of others.

Matthew 10:16 (NKJV) "Behold, I send you out as sheep in the midst of wolves. Therefore be wise as serpents and harmless as doves."

It seems that a lot of Christians have this verse backwards; they are as harmless as serpents and as wise as doves.

We will always do better when we fit ourselves into God's plan than when we try to fit God into our plan.

In 2 Corinthians 2:14 Paul wrote, "Now thanks be to God who always leads us in triumph in Christ ..."

Many Christians like this verse, but they don't always like the fact that to "triumph" you first must have a situation to overcome and be victorious in.

Living a life of victory does not mean you will never face a challenge.

Next time you face a difficult situation, just look at it in the light of this verse and allow the Holy Spirit to lead you in the way you should go and follow His direction into your triumph!

See if you notice anything about these equations.

2 + 2 = 3
2 + 2 = 4
2 + 2 = 5

These are not three equally valid opinions. One is true and the other two are false.

2 + 2 = 4 in all situations, it is not different for different people, it is simply a fact that you can choose to accept or reject.

There is truth and there are opinions.

Truth does not change based on opinions, but opinions can change when the truth is found.

John 8:32 (NKJV) "And you shall know the truth, and the truth shall make you free."

Jesus said that knowing the truth, knowing God's Word, would make us free.

Jesus did not say that if we know the Word we would be depressed or put into bondage.

If we hear teaching that brings fear, confusion, or discouragement then we are not hearing teaching based on the Word of God.

No matter who you are or where you come from, sometime in your life you will meet someone who dislikes you for your background, your skin color, your education level, your ethnic heritage, or some other thing.

We have the choice of whether or not we are going to allow some other person's perception of us to be what defines us; it is much better for us to find out who we are in God's sight and live our life based on that.

Find your identity in God's Word and don't let others shape you by their words and ideas.

Our spiritual location is far more important than our geographic location.

Proverbs 19:20 (NKJV) "Listen to counsel and receive instruction, that you may be wise in your latter days."

God will give us counsel, instruction, and correction today, through His Word and by the Holy Spirit, to prepare us for our future.

It is wise to take time to listen to God today so that we will know what to do tomorrow.

It does not matter what someone wrote in a book or said in some teaching somewhere, no matter how logical it sounds or how wonderful it makes you feel, if it does not agree with what you find in the Bible then forget it and stay with the Bible!

You will be much, much better off if you do.

James 1:21-22 (NKJV) "Therefore lay aside all filthiness and overflow of wickedness, and receive with meekness the implanted word, which is able to save your souls. But be doers of the word, and not hearers only, deceiving yourselves."

We are told to receive the Word and then to do the Word; that is the formula for a successful life.

But, it seems like a lot of people think that James 1 says: "see where you can agree with the Word and do it if you want to and if you feel like it". That is a formula for failure.

One word spoken as directed by the Holy Spirit will be more effective than 100 words spoken from our own understanding.

Acting like the Bible does not say something you dislike is a bit like the child who thinks people disappear when the child shuts their eyes.

Sometimes we just need to accept what the Bible says and make the change; God will help us if we let Him.

It's better to accept the truth and adjust ourselves to it than to walk around with your spiritual eyes shut and continue bumping into things that are "not there".

You can have facts in your head without having any truth in your heart.

Receive and believe the truth and then act on it, don't let it just get stuck in your head.

Too often Christians try to rely on intellectual means to define and understand spiritual truth.

This leads to wrong doctrine and confusion.

Using Scripture to interpret other Scripture is a better method than just using your mind to interpret Scripture.

Some people seem to think that the way to prove a doctrine is by checking to see if it agrees with what they already think or how it makes them feel.

The only way to build sound doctrine is that it first and foremost comes from God's Word

There are a lot of people who are waiting for God to do something in their life to give them success, to show them what to do, or to have a change in their life.

God gave us His Son Jesus, God gave us His Word, and God gave us the Holy Spirit.

Instead of our waiting for God to do something else maybe we should start doing something with all of the things that has God already given us.

Too many Christians minimize God's Word while maximizing intellect, emotions, or experiences.

Although intellect, emotions, and experiences are not necessarily bad, we cannot base our life on them. But, we can and should base our life on the Word of God.

John 8:31-32 (NKJV) "Then Jesus said to those Jews who believed Him, "If you abide in My word, you are My disciples indeed. And you shall know the truth, and the truth shall make you free."

Jesus did not say, "just hear something once and forget it", or "accept the truth if you want to and if it fits into your life", or "you believe whatever you want and be My disciple", or "the truth will always make you more comfortable", or "you will be free anyway no matter what you do".

Jesus said, "If you abide in My Word, you are my disciples indeed. And you shall know the truth and the truth shall make you free".

God's Word will produce results in our life when we stay in it, know it, and act on it.

God's Word does not produce results if we do not put it into practice the way we should.

The latest clever phrase that our favorite minister/pastor/teacher, or whoever, came up with is not on the same level as God's Word.

We must all check everything we hear through the filter of the Word of God to see if it really is biblical.

Ignorance is not a fruit of the Spirit.

God wants us to grow and develop in our knowledge and our understanding of Him and His Word.

Every individual that makes up a team in a local church is an important part of that team.

Every team in the local church is an important part of that church.

Every local church is an important part of God's plan.

Every local church, every team within that local church, and every person on a team are all an important part of God's will being fulfilled on the earth. It is up to all of us to do our part in God's plan.

The words, the wisdom, and the way to go all come from God.

He guides, He provides, He directs.

Our part is to recognize those things and then obey.

Our timetable and God's are usually not the same. We are often in more of a hurry to do things than God is or than we actually need to be.

To be most effective in what we are doing we must do it in God's timing.

Just because we know what to do does not mean we have to do it immediately. Just because we have a plan does not mean that it will come to pass tomorrow.

It is wise to be sure that what we do is done in God's timing and not in our timing.

Isaiah 26:3 (NKJV) "You will keep him in perfect peace, whose mind is stayed on You, because he trusts in You."

If someone is not living in peace, then it is certain that their mind is not focused on God and His Word.

If we want the perfect kind of peace that only God can offer, then we need to keep our thoughts focused on Him, trusting in Him.

If we are in a state of mental turmoil and emotional distress, we have put our mind on something other than God and His Word.

External, natural circumstances do not change spiritual truths.

But, spiritual truths can change external, natural circumstances.

Isaiah 40:8 (NKJV) "The grass withers, the flower fades, But the word of our God stands forever."

There are a lot of things that change in this world: the weather, seasons, popular viewpoints, styles, political leaders, etc. etc.

It is good to know that God and His Word do not change; God's Word is where we can find true stability and security in an ever changing, unstable world.

Sundays, and while at other church meetings or services, should not be the only time Christians read their Bibles, pray, praise, worship, and serve God.

These are all things that should be done as a regular part of the life of a believer, to help them develop and maintain a strong and stable walk with the Lord.

The Christian life is not a constant struggle of trying to get to some place to get something.

The Christian life is about finding out who we are in Christ and what belongs to us in Christ, and staying in that place no matter what tries to move us away.

God has a plan for each and every person, and He has given everyone some gift and ability to use to glorify Him and serve others.

Our task is to discover that gift and ability from God and then to make the best use of it as God directs us.

Ecclesiastes 9:17 (NKJV) "Words of the wise, spoken quietly, should be heard rather than the shout of a ruler of fools."

Sometimes the things that are said quietly and that don't get a lot of attention are more important and true than things that are loudly proclaimed by many people.

Just because a lot of people say, or even repeat something, does not mean that it is right, true, or good.

Romans 12:2 (NKJV) "And do not be conformed to this world, but be transformed by the renewing of your mind, that you may prove what is that good and acceptable and perfect will of God."

A person is either being transformed by the renewing of their mind or they are being conformed to the world.

If you don't get transformed, you will be conformed and the result will be that you are deformed.

If you are transformed, you will be reformed and the result will be that you are shaped into God's norm.

By just listening to what some ministers teach, you would think that there was no New Testament/New Covenant because everything they say seems to be from the Old Testament.

Certainly, the Old Testament is valuable to us today and we can use Old Testament verses and principles in our teaching and in our life, but we cannot solely use the Old Testament while ignoring what we see in the New Testament.

We have to base what we teach and believe primarily on the New Testament/New Covenant.

Some people have beliefs and build doctrines that are shaped by the experiences of the past and their upbringing.

If we are for or against something, we need to have clear Scripture to back up our beliefs or we are living a life built on the wrong foundation.

Our foundation in life needs to be God's Word, that is the only stable, sure foundation.

What is being said, the content of the message, is more important than who is actually speaking.

If we are only impressed with who is speaking and not really listening to what is being said we can find ourselves in trouble in many ways.

Some people approach the Bible with preconceived ideas and try to find something in the Bible that agrees with what they already believe, think, feel, do, and say.

The correct approach to the Bible is that we allow what God says to us in His Word to shape our beliefs, thoughts, attitudes, actions, and words.

Matthew 7:7-8 (NKJV) "Ask, and it will be given to you; seek, and you will find; knock, and it will be opened to you. For everyone who asks receives, and he who seeks finds, and to him who knocks it will be opened."

This is a simple truth, but it is also sometimes misunderstood.

If we ask and want to receive, we have to ask for the right thing. If I want a drink of water I can't ask for a piece of bread and expect the right result.

If we seek and want to find, we have to be looking for the right thing in the right place. If I want to find the Eifel Tower I can't seek for The Great Wall of China.

If we knock and want something to be opened, we have to knock in the right place. I can knock on the wall all I want, but unless I knock on a door nothing will open.

We have to ask, seek, and knock correctly to get the right results.

Integrity, meaning uprightness in character and action, incorruptibility, trustworthiness, and honesty, should be more than just a word we find in the dictionary, especially for Christians.

Just because you are doing something does not mean it is something worth doing.

There are a lot of things that believers do that take up a lot of their time, but those things do not always help their spiritual development.

Activity and spirituality are not necessarily the same thing.

Proverbs 16:9 (NKJV) "A man's heart plans his way, but the Lord directs his steps."

Proverbs 19:21 (NKJV) "There are many plans in a man's heart, Nevertheless the Lord's counsel - that will stand."

Often people have an idea, even from God, but they don't allow God to guide their steps in that plan as to how and when to put the plan into action.

Trying to use our own wisdom to bring the plans in our heart to pass will lead to failure.

We must get wisdom and counsel from God for everything that we are doing.

Following God's direction concerning the plans in our heart will lead to successful completion of the plan.

If we continue to walk in the light that God has already given us in His Word and through the Holy Spirit, then as we need more light, wisdom, and direction it will come.

If we do not walk in the light that we do have and don't follow the direction and wisdom that God has given us, then we will not necessarily get more light or understanding.

The key is to do what we know to do and not just focus on what we don't know yet.

The answers we need are not in our head, so it would probably be a good idea to stop looking to our own understanding to figure everything out.

We need to look to God and the wisdom and direction He will give us through the Bible and the Holy Spirit.

By following the Word of God and the Holy Spirit we will have the answers we need every time.

Rather than just sit and wonder about all of the things that are not clear to us and that we don't understand in the Bible, we need to act on what we do see clearly and do understand.

Just because you think it, does not mean you have to say it or do it.

Buildings start with a blueprint, the plan for how the building should be built.

For any building to be built successfully, and function the way it should, the building would have to be made according to the blueprint.

The New Testament is like a blueprint for the Christian life.

Your present position is not an accurate indication of your future destination.

It may be, but it doesn't have to be.

The right thing to do is always the right thing to do, no matter how we feel about it, if it does or does not directly benefit us personally, and no matter who says it is right or not.

If it is the right thing to do, then it is the right thing to do.

Today and tomorrow are two different days. Some things are for today and some things are for tomorrow. The different things to be done on each of those days needs to be clear.

You can't do things tomorrow that must be done today, and there are some things you cannot do today that will have to be done tomorrow.

By following the leading of the Holy Spirit, and using wisdom, we can keep today's things in perspective and keep tomorrow's things in their proper time, so that we do everything at the right time, all of the time.

Luke 4:16 (NKJV) "So He came to Nazareth, where He had been brought up. And as His custom was, He went into the synagogue on the Sabbath day, and stood up to read."

It was Jesus custom to go to the Synagogue, it was something He had a practice of doing, it was a regular part of His life. This would be equivalent to Christians having the habit of going to church regularly.

Since this was something Jesus was accustomed to doing, I wonder if it would also be a good habit for us to have. People talk about being like Jesus and following the pattern He left us, this would be a good place to start.

Proverbs 9:12 (NKJV) "If you are wise, you are wise for yourself, and if you scoff, you will bear it alone. "

Too many people want someone else to be wise for them, to spend the time doing the right things for them and learning what is necessary to be successful in life instead of doing it themselves.

If you are wise you will be the primary beneficiary of the wisdom you gain and in a good position to help others.

If you are a "scoffer" you will reap the consequences; it is really your choice, your responsibility, it is up to you, not someone else.

According to the Bible, if we put God first, the things we need, and even the desires of our heart, will come to us. (Matthew 6:33; Psalm 37:4).

God's plan for us is to have a happy, blessed, successful, wonderful life. But, our goal in life is not just to have a happy life.

Our goal in life should be to fulfill the will of God. As we follow God and do His will, all the things we need and desire, including a happy life, will be added to us.

We cannot control everything that happens in our life, but we can control how we respond to the things that happen.

Psalm 37:5 (NKJV) "Commit your way to the Lord, trust also in Him, and He shall bring it to pass."

When God gives us ideas, dreams, and plans we sometimes try to make things happen on our own.

But we need to trust God and follow His direction about the ideas, dreams, and plans that we have.

God will bring us opportunities that we could not make happen for ourselves and He will open doors for us that others could not, or would not, open for us.

Our part is to trust God and follow Him, and He will bring it to pass.

People often value talent and ability over character and faithfulness; God always values character and faithfulness over talent and ability.

Deuteronomy 29:29 (NKJV) "The secret things belong to the LORD our God, but those things which are revealed belong to us and to our children forever, that we may do all the words of this law.

We can always ask ourselves, "What has God revealed to me in His Word about my life and my current situation?" It is what God has revealed to us that we need to focus on and do.

God is big enough to see ahead in our life and smart enough to prepare us for what we will face in the future.

We usually don't need to go look for some new revelation or a new answer, we just need to see what God has already revealed to us and then act on it.

If we want to build a successful life we must build our life according to the blueprint that God has given us in His Word, especially the New Testament.

God's plan is not just a part of our life, it is our life.